Of Course
It Hurts

 FriesenPress

Suite 300 - 990 Fort St
Victoria, BC, V8V 3K2
Canada

www.friesenpress.com

ISBN
978-1-5255-3617-5 (Hardcover)
978-1-5255-3618-2 (Paperback)
978-1-5255-3619-9 (eBook)

1. *Poetry, Subjects & Themes, Death, Grief, Loss*

Distributed to the trade by The Ingram Book Company

Of Course It Hurts

Brett Elena

Of course it hurts, darling.

Of course it stings and cracks and
whips and roars.

It fills your head with whispers
and your room with angry silence.
Crouching, unwanted, unwelcome.

Like a shadow two steps behind.

Don't let anyone ever tell you
That it's
"all right."

Sometimes things,
well, they aren't "all right."

In fact,

they can be downright squirrely

and that's perfectly natural.
In fact, it's expected,

like sunsets, Black Friday sales,
and horrendous Dad jokes.

You're allowed to admit you're hurt.

You're allowed to
talk about pain.

It doesn't make you weak. It makes you
real. And also,

it's a darn good excuse for more hugs.

And hugs are awesome. At any age.

(This is a puppy who loves hugs.)

By the way . . .

Warm fuzzies are awesome at any age, too.
Because you're never too old to need love

. . . or naps . . . or funnel cakes . . . or appreciation.

(This most dignified señor proves age never
holds back fun.)

(She looks like she's enjoying herself a lot more than the homebound gamers, too.)

Of course you can be sad, my dear.

Sometimes you will be.

Some days, you won't want to get out
of bed.

The effort of moving
will just seem too much.

Sometimes the sadness takes shape,

like a purple, furry monster
with bedazzled pink horns
and leathery wings.

It sits in the corner
and refuses to leave.

Uninvited, unasked-for.

Miserable and time-devouring.

It's not pretty

and it doesn't sing the blues.

And you never see red, puffy, and
tear-stained eyes

in this week's copy of *Vogue*.

And that's perfectly natural, too

(because *Vogue* somehow,
mysteriously, forgot EVERY SINGLE
PERSON's reality).

A splash of different, of off-color, of

broken . . .

makes it all a little more . . .

believeable.

So own your sorrow, dear one.

Embrace every single drop.

No one can tell you

how you "should" feel.

Or how the "normal" response appears

(though they may feel hideous, I
promise: each tear is a miniscule,
crystalline wonder).

Another fun fact:

Of course you can scowl.
You don't *need* to smile.

Not for anyone. Not for your boss, not
for your friends (though they might
sneakily bust it out of your/Superman's
Fortress of Solitude).

You don't *need* to be charming.

You don't *need* to be on 100% of
the time.

Actually, I would probably be alarmed
if you were.

What is this, Stepford?

Smile because you're happy.

Laugh because the mirth bubbles over
(and you can't help its escape).

Grin because mischief won out
or the puppy had a bowtie
(same same).

Don't ever smile because you "have to"
or it's "expected."

You don't.

Those expectations,

they're wrong.

The boy-/girl-next-door

/Miss Venezuela/ Peter Pan/

The jellified-knees, instant-stammer,
unbearably cute grocery clerk.

I bet sometimes they glare, too.

Because it's human.

Because it's real.

You don't need to pretend you're a
preternaturally perky saint

just to get a date.

(The right person always appreciates
your truth, doncha know.)

(Smiling Gingy the Gingerbread Man—but
only because he felt like it!)

(Giant lumberjack mural men only smile when inspired, too.)

For the record, sweet child,
of course bad hair days go down.

(insert ANY of my bedhead
mirror pics)

Sometimes, yes,
you will have a nest
instead of a 'do.

(A nest/nightmare/trainwreck.)

Or that cowlick becomes permanent.
Or the hairspray goes awry.
Or your comb disappears.
Or allllllllll your hair ties break.

And every curl, every strand,
every lock
decides to come into
an implacable, nonnegotiable,
no-quarters-given

State of Rebellion.

You are still beautiful.

In fact, you are ALWAYS beautiful.

I truly hope you realize that.

Forget the magazines.
Forget the dolls and commercials
and the done-up, made-up
"real" people on TV.

It is literally their job to look good.

And they have a whole team to make
that happen.

But YOU. Yes, you.
You. Are. Beautiful.

Because, really, beauty is quite different from your appearance.

(I mean, of course your freckles
are art, and that grin would melt
the Grinch,

but beauty is something different.
Something deeper.)

Beauty is empathy. Beauty
is gratitude.
Beauty is acknowledging your
mother's sacrifices
or noticing the everyday divine.

Beauty is your sleepy, barely
there yawn.

Or your racing hurry at rest.

It's helping your neighbor
(/brother/sister/frenemy).

Beauty is encouraging those forgotten
or helping up the fallen.

Beauty is strength; beauty is soul.

Beauty is choosing to hold on—
always.

It's open-mic sashaying
at your 5:00 am, radio
pop, way-too-loud
solo sing-along.

Beauty has very little to do with how
you look
and everything to do with your heart.

People are most beautiful

doing what they love.

For the record, though . . .

of course you're going to get mad.

Not every day is rainbows.
Of course you will rage. And scream.

And, shucks, maybe throw a pout in,
too.

And you won't always know why.

Or you'll say things you don't mean
and seem far crueler than intended.

And self-doubt?

Well, some days—you know,
THOSE days—
it's stickier than pecan pie.

It happens.

It happens to everyone,
not just you.

Forgive others their biting,
unkind moments.

Forgive yourself, too.

Sometimes, "one step at a time"

means tripping three steps backward

. . . twice. In a row.

And that is 100% <u>okay</u>.

Honor yourself for the process.
For the progress.

For braving the risk of each
faltering step.

And when (not if) you fall,

Just make the experience useful and
learn something—about yourself,
about your reactions, about others.

See, if we had no cracks,
how would light get in?

(That's paraphrasing Leonard
Cohen, by the way. He was a pretty
cool dude.)

(Light)

(More light, coming through cracks!)

(Shadow-healing New Zealand
sunset light.)

(Also, side exercise: Stop reading and write three things about yourself that you love.)

1. _____

2. _____

3. _____

(Definitely wasn't kidding. Add a
bonus 4 and 5!)

"Compassion"

Kind of trite, isn't it?

Over-used, over-abused,
Excellent guilt material.

But *habibti*

(that's Arabic for "my love.")

Compassion just means recognizing
<u>we are all in this together.</u>
"The others"/Boo Radley/the Wicked
Witch/the Yankees
are just friends we haven't met.

(Nepalese chickens playing together.)

(British people dancing—
also together!)

Of course it seems overwhelming.

Of course it feels like a disaster,

a shambles,

like everything is wrong or unfair

and, frankly, downright scary.

It could be the news; it could be a
test. It could be family fighting non-
stop, even though
they say they "love you."

(They really do, though.
Sometimes they
simply aren't the best at showing it.
Because the dirty secret is,
they're human, too.)

Stress is like an evil,
omnipresent jackalope

that pops up at the worst times
in all the wrong places. For whatever
reason—real, made-up, sugar-
binge hallucination.

But . . .

chin up, my love.

There is always grace to be found,
in the most unexpected of places,
at the most unlikely of moments,
from the most bizarre of sources.

You see, grace is kind of like confetti .
. . or glitter . . . or magical pixie dust.
It. Is. Literally.
EVERYWHERE.
AT ALL TIMES.
ALWAYS.
AND IT DOESN'T GO AWAY.

Grace for you. Grace for me. Grace
for everyone.
Not because we did anything to
earn it,

but because you are you.

and you deserve good things.

Time.

It's a son of a gun, isn't it?
Those glorious summers race on by,
but sometimes time drags, like when
things are tough. Or nerve-wracking.
Or, you know, suuuuuuper annoying.

(It especially seems to drag when
things are tough.)

I know, because I've been there. I have
stared at the clock, willing the second
hand to move a smidgen faster, just
a tad,
if only to finish what feels like an
endless, pointless "game."

Sometimes it feels like the Gods
are tipsy,
playing Chinese checkers with our
life stories.

But keep the faith, dear one.
One more second, one more minute, one
more hour, one more day.

Keep the faith.

"It is the way of all things that the night ends and light returns.
The light always returns."
—Brian Andreas

(He's a pretty cool compadre, too.)

And, like I said . . .

hugs are awesome
and they make everything better.

(Lots and lots of blankets/tent forts
are also AWESOME.)

A Checklist

If you have:

1. Shoes on your feet

2. A roof over your head

3. Security that you will still be breathing in the morning/no bombing, shelling, violent crime

4. ONE person who cares. Just one

5. A heartbeat that doesn't quit

6. Food in your belly

7. A guaranteed source of clean water

THEN YOU ARE BEYOND BLESSED.

It's all about perspective.

"Patience, young grasshopper." **

** Mr. Miyagi quote, 1984, "The Karate Kid." If you haven't seen it, you totally need to drop everything now and go watch it... well, why are you still reading?! Go! Run! Run, Forrest, run! (Yes, that is a mixed movie reference, and I defy anyone's disapproval. You can write your own book with proper, singular-cinema citations.)

As big as your school may seem,
as vast as its role looms in your
everyday life,
I promise,
your elementary, middle, and high
schools combined, times ten (plus the
pre-school playground!)
are just a very, very small corner of a
very, very wide world.

And if you don't like your current reality,
CHANGE IT.

With DARING,
BOLDNESS,
and VISION.

You are only ever as "stuck" as you allow yourself to be.

No walls are eternal
while starlight yet gleams.

Of course you should speak up, m'dear.

Say exactly what you feel needs to be said.

Let your voice ring out.

Write down your memories.

Commit your spirit.

You were given a voice for a reason.

And a mind, too.

It's not "dumb" to miss people.

It's not a waste of time.

It's not "childish" to

hold conversations

with those closest to our hearts—

WHEREVER their current address:

the sky, the ocean, Illinois.

Loneliness is not the fictitious whim of
Dr. Phil's next guest.
It shows
you're human.
It shows
you remember your soul.

You remember who you are

and crave real connection.

And, frankly,

that's commendable.

See, people, well, we're
finicky creatures.
We like to pretend we are intense
and fierce and all individualist and
lonesome and strong
. . . or whatever.

We're not.

We need each other. It's just a simple
truth, like Saturday morning cartoons.

Or ice cream.

Or watercolor palettes.

Or wool sweaters, scarves, and hot
cocoa in winter...

Point being, it's a thing.

So, LOVE LOUD.
LOVE NOW.

Vulnerability IS strength.
It's true, our clumsy clay feet may
lead to

some bumps and bruises along the way,

But please don't—
don't lose an opportunity to reach out.
To engage.

Please don't—
Don't forget the healing comfort
of just a simple call.

So, for me, little one, please
shuck off your pride,
push through your hesitation,

and tell your friends how much
they matter;
what a difference they make.

(Buddhism teaches the connectedness of the whole—the air we breathe, the ground, the sheltering light.

Their fluttering prayer flags spread
goodwill on the wings of the wind.)

"Issues."

"Insecurities."

"Flaws."

We've all got them.
The rich kids, the popular ones,
the supposed-savants,
and the teachers' pets.

Don't ever put yourself down
because you think you're "less than."

Each woman/child/caribou has their
own path
and their own hidden struggles.

"Carefree, happy-go lucky, has-it-all."

They're just myths and lies we
tell ourselves

to salt self-inflicted wounds.

Don't.

stop.

Breathe.

Don't do that to yourself.

Sometimes we make mistakes.

But we are all cherished,

We are all

imperfectly perfect.

And if you're confused or frustrated or upset . . .

well, I probably am, too. Or maybe not
(unlikely—we all cry a lot more than
we admit).
(Which is super-duper okay, too! It's
called progress.)
(While Fergie's "Big Girls Don't Cry" is
a dope song, it's totally untrue. All of
the big kids cry—the girls, the guys,
Casper the Friendly Ghost. ERRBODY.)

The important thing is,

you are not alone

(. . . ever).

(See, even polar bears come to
say "hello"

and to remind you that you're great.)

Of course you should do what makes you happy.

Whatever it is.

Piano, gymnastics,

riding, rock-collecting,

yoga, running, knitting, crocheting,

cataloging trees,

ornithology.

(Photography.)

(Skateboarding.)

(Fishing.)

It could be anything. Find a way.
If there are obstacles, get creative.
Even if
some people find it "weird"
or "nerdy" or "odd."

Ignore them. This is your life,
not theirs,

and you deserve happiness.

Of course words break harder than
sticks and stones.
Believe me, cariño, I know it.
I've felt that cruel, unjust whip.

Words that crackle, words that snap.
Words tap dancing across
malicious half-truths
for seemingly no reason at all.

I know their echo reverbs and grows.

But try not to listen
(they're reflections of their
limitations, not yours).
(For you were born of joy and for joy.
And you were made to shine.)

So,

I guess what I'm trying to say is . . .

love yourself.

Love yourself enough to be hurt.
Love yourself enough to acknowledge
that hurt and not hide it away.

Record forever your yesterdays and
todays and dreams for tomorrow.

Paint your home, what centers you.
What cuts. Remember these truths.
They are yours.

Don't be swayed by some fickle
"in-crowd" (who decides who's "in"
anyway? What does that even mean?).

Be kind.

Make peace with your quirks.

Call a truce with shame.

Accept your grief.

Accept your anger.

Accept your stuttering, stumbling,
perpetually late,

mind-blowingly AMAZING humanity.

Don't fight against an ideal that doesn't exist.

Just be you.

And love one another.

Every hour

of every day.

(Always.)